THE LIBRARY OF
MEDIEVAL TIMES

Medieval Warfare

Don Nardo

ReferencePoint
Press®

San Diego, CA

© 2015 ReferencePoint Press, Inc.
Printed in the United States

For more information, contact:
ReferencePoint Press, Inc.
PO Box 27779
San Diego, CA 92198
www. ReferencePointPress.com

ALL RIGHTS RESERVED.
No part of this work covered by the copyright hereon may be reproduced or used in any form or by any means—graphic, electronic, or mechanical, including photocopying, recording, taping, web distribution, or information storage retrieval systems—without the written permission of the publisher.

LIBRARY OF CONGRESS CATALOGING-IN-PUBLICATION DATA

Nardo, Don, 1947-
  Medieval warfare / by Don Nardo.
    pages cm. -- (Library of medieval times)
  Includes bibliographical references and index.
  ISBN-13: 978-1-60152-682-3 (hardback)
  ISBN-10: 1-60152-682-2 (hardback)
  1. Military art and science--History--Medieval, 500-1500. 2. Military history, Medieval. I. Title.
  U37.N368 2015
  355.0209'02--dc23

                                 2013050194

355.02 NAR   OCT 0 4 2014
Nardo, Don

Medieval warfare

HUDSON PUBLIC LIBRARY
3 WASHINGTON ST
@WOOD SQUARE
HUDSON, MA 01749

PLEASE
DO NOT REMOVE
CARD
FROM POCKET

CONTENTS

IMPORTANT EVENTS OF MEDIEVAL TIMES

800
In Rome, Pope Leo III crowns Charlemagne emperor; his Carolingian dynasty rules western Europe until 987.

1000
A century of invention in farming begins; devices such as the heavy plow increase agricultural productivity and help double Europe's population.

632
The Prophet Muhammad dies as Islam begins to expand both east and west of the Arabian Peninsula.

ca. 950
Europe's first medical school opens in Salerno, Italy.

1099
The First Crusade ends Muslim rule in Jerusalem until 1187, when the Muslims under Saladin recapture Jerusalem from the Crusaders.

400   600   800   1000   1200

476
Romulus Augustulus, the last Roman emperor in the West, is dethroned.

1066
William of Normandy defeats the last Anglo-Saxon king at the Battle of Hastings, establishing Norman rule in England.

1200
The rise of universities begins to promote a revival of learning throughout the West.

1130
Church authorities in France ban tournaments; the ban on these popular festivals, which provide knights with opportunities to gain prestige and financial reward, is later reversed.

1184
Church officials meeting in Verona, Italy, approve burning at the stake as a punishment for anyone found guilty of heresy.

1215
King John of England signs the Magna Carta, limiting the rights of the monarchy.

1346
Using the longbow, English archers overwhelm the French army at the Battle of Crécy during the Hundred Years' War.

1328
Charles IV dies, ending 341 years of successful rule by the Capetian kings who established modern France.

1316
The Italian physician Mondino De' Luzzi writes the first book of the medieval period devoted entirely to anatomy.

1378
The Great Schism, in which there are three claimants to the papacy, occurs.

| 1250 | 1300 | 1350 | 1400 | 1450 |

1347
The deadly bubonic plague strikes Europe and returns intermittently for the next 250 years.

1337
The Hundred Years' War begins between France and England.

1453
The Ottoman Turks conquer Constantinople following a seven-week bombardment with cannons.

1267
Henry III of England enacts the Assize of Bread and Ale, one of the first laws to regulate the production and sale of food; the law ties the price of bread to the price of wheat, thus preventing bakers from setting artificially high prices.

1231
Pope Gregory IX establishes the "Holy Inquisition," whose purpose is to search out heretics and force them to renounce their views.

Medieval Warfare Transformed

On Saturday, October 14, 1066, the rays of the early morning sun revealed a dramatic scene near England's southern coast. Approximately eight thousand Englishmen, called Saxons, had gathered in an open field about 7 miles (11 km) northwest of the coastal town of Hastings. The mood among these men was solemn, and many of them wore grim looks. All were carrying weapons, and those who could afford it were decked out in chain mail and other kinds of armor.

These warriors had carefully lined up across the field, standing in ranks, one behind another, in preparation for a bloody battle. Each was well aware that he might be among those unfortunate individuals who would be lying dead a few hours later, and fear was in the air. Hoping for reassurance, some of the soldiers looked toward their leader. A tall, handsome man in his mid-forties—and known for his formidable fighting skills—stood, his expression determined, beside the national banners atop a low hill in the center of the field. He was King Harold II. Less than nine months before, he had ascended the throne upon the death of the former Saxon ruler, Edward the Confessor.

Gazing out across the meadows, Harold could see the crowded ranks of the opposing army arrayed directly in front of his own forces. A large proportion of the enemy fighters were cavalry (mounted warriors). It was clear that they would soon push forward and attack the lines of his infantry (foot soldiers), who he hoped would be able to hold their ground and keep the invaders from winning the day.

Harold and his troops viewed their opponents as invaders for good reason. These adversaries had recently crossed the English Channel with the intention of conquering Saxon England. Their leader, William, Duke of Normandy (in northwest France), believed that he, not Harold, was the rightful heir to Edward's throne, and he had come to claim it.

After gathering a Norman army at least as large as Harold's, William had loaded his forces onto small ships, crossed the channel, and landed at Pevensey, on the English coast several miles southwest of Hastings. His spies had told him that Harold's army was approaching the area, so the duke had hastily marched his own forces northeastward. He had no way of knowing that the ensuing encounter would turn out to be one of the largest and most fateful battles of Europe's medieval era.

"Ut, ut, ut!"

According to one medieval source, just before the start of the Battle of Hastings a single Norman rode out and stopped in the empty no-man's-land stretching between the opposing armies. An entertainer known for his juggling skills, that rider, Taillefer by name, began taunting the enemy fighters. Repeatedly, he expertly juggled his sword, tossing it up into the air and catching it by the handle, each time escaping injury from the sharpened blade. Enraged at this display, a lone Saxon soldier lost his temper and ran out to attack Taillefer. What the Englishman did not realize was that the juggler was also an accomplished warrior. As the assailant approached him, he swiftly plucked his sword from the air and swung it sideways with tremendous force. The blade separated the other man's head from his body, which collapsed to the ground with a dull thud.

The sight of this gruesome but impressive feat filled the Normans with confidence. Duke William nodded at his trumpeter, who sounded a series of loud blasts, the signal for the charge, and the Norman ranks surged forward. Awaiting the oncoming enemy, the men in the Saxon lines raised loud battle cries. "Godemite!" ("God Almighty!"), they shouted, and then began chanting "Ut, ut, ut!" ("Out, out, out!").[1]

Hails of Norman arrows showered the first few rows of Saxon soldiers. But the men raised their wooden, leather-covered shields, which stopped many of the arrows in mid-flight. So Saxon losses to the Norman archers

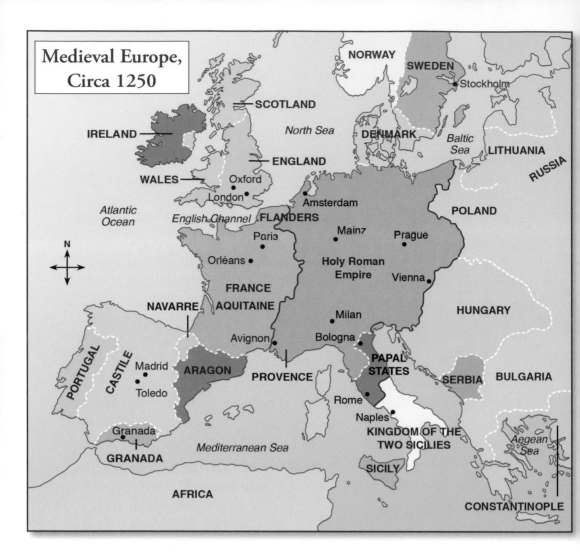

Medieval Europe, Circa 1250

NORWAY

SWEDEN

Stockholm

SCOTLAND

North Sea

DENMARK

Baltic Sea

LITHUANIA

IRELAND

RUSSIA

ENGLAND

WALES

Oxford

London

Amsterdam

POLAND

Atlantic Ocean

English Channel

FLANDERS

Mainz

Prague

Paris

Orléans

Holy Roman Empire

Vienna

FRANCE

NAVARRE

AQUITAINE

HUNGARY

Milan

Avignon

Bologna

PAPAL STATES

Madrid

ARAGON

PROVENCE

SERBIA

BULGARIA

Toledo

Rome

Naples

Granada

KINGDOM OF THE TWO SICILIES

Aegean Sea

GRANADA

Mediterranean Sea

SICILY

AFRICA

CONSTANTINOPLE

N

were few. Seconds later, the initial horde of Norman horsemen crashed into the front Saxon line, driving it backward several feet. Yet though a number of men in that rank were skewered on Norman lances and swords, soldiers from the second Saxon rank immediately leaped forward and took their places. As a result, the line largely held. Moreover, the men in the first several Saxon ranks hurled javelins and rocks at the mounted Normans, killing or maiming dozens of them. In the words of British military historian Christopher Gravett, "The clash of weapons, the shrieks of the wounded men and horses, together with the shouting and chanting of those at the rear must have been appalling as the knights spurred their horses towards the mêlée. As they did so, they too were struck by missiles that tumbled them to the ground or maddened their horses."[2]

"The Dropping of the Dead"

Despite the deaths of some of his cavalrymen, in the hours that followed William ordered charge after bloody charge against the English ranks. But though they suffered heavy losses, the brave Saxon infantry held firm. French priest and historian William of Poitiers, who personally knew and served Duke William, later described this stage of the battle. "Where one side works by constant motion and ceaseless charges," he wrote, "the other can but endure passively as it stands fixed to the sod. The Norman arrow and sword worked on. In the English ranks the only movement was the dropping of the dead. The living stood motionless."[3]

Seeing that the cavalry charges alone were not forceful enough to break the enemy lines, William finally tried a different strategy. He had his horsemen pretend to retreat down the hillside. Sure enough, just as he had hoped, many of the Saxons broke ranks and chased after the Norman riders. That left big gaps in the Saxon lines into which other Norman fighters rushed. Eventually, King Harold's infantry ranks fell apart, and the onrushing Norman forces approached him and his personal bodyguards at the hill's summit. According to some sources, as these guards met their deaths around him, he fought on courageously, killing numerous Normans before an arrow entered one of his eyes and penetrated his brain. (In recent years, a number of modern scholars have disputed this, saying that the Saxon monarch may have died in some other manner.)

> **WORDS IN CONTEXT**
>
> **mêlée: Rowdy fight or military clash, usually involving at least several combatants.**

At this point, according to William of Poitiers, the remaining Saxon soldiers "realized beyond doubt that they could no longer stand against the Normans. They knew that they were reduced by heavy losses and that the king himself, with his brothers and many nobles of the realm, had fallen." Therefore, they "turned to flight and made off as soon as they got the chance."[4]

A Prolific and Vigorous Builder

The death of their king, along with the loss of numerous nobles and well-trained warriors, demoralized the Saxons. This greatly aided William and his plan to gain the throne he felt was rightfully his. Moving northward from the coast, he methodically orchestrated his conquest, relatively quickly turning England into a Norman-controlled nation.

Together, the Battle of Hastings and the Norman Conquest that followed marked a turning point, not only in England's history, but also in the development of medieval warfare. In large part this was because the conqueror, William, perfected the use of one of the chief defensive and offensive military devices of that era in Europe—the castle. He did not invent castles—various versions of these structures existed in the Middle East and elsewhere in ancient times. However, William was the first European ruler to demonstrate the military effectiveness of the widespread use of castles, especially the stone variety.

WORDS IN CONTEXT

motte and bailey: Early, crude form of castle made of earth, wood, and other easily obtained and largely perishable materials.

William was a prolific and vigorous castle builder. Almost immediately after securing England's southern region late in 1066, he set gangs of laborers to work erecting castles across the captured countryside. Called motte and baileys, these were small and crude by later standards, yet they were extremely successful in maintaining military control of the conquered regions.

Each of these structures consisted of two principal parts. The first, the motte, was a mound of earth averaging from 30 to 60 feet (9 to 18 m) high. Builders erected a wooden tower atop the mound and surrounded it with a sturdy wooden stockade fence. The fence ran down the hillside and widened into a protected enclosure, the bailey, at ground level. "Capable of quick construction of plentiful materials by largely unskilled labor," military historian Archer Jones remarks, a motte and bailey "offered a powerful defense against attackers who had little experience in sieges. Thus, these crude castles provided a base for operations, dominated the country around them, and provided a place of refuge for the conquerors in time of trouble."[5]

Into the History Books

William built hundreds of motte and bailey castles in the first few years he ruled England. Once he was satisfied that his control of the country was secure, he took the next crucial step in castle evolution—rebuilding those earthen and wooden fortifications, only this time using stronger and more permanent stone. Rulers and members of the nobility, not only in the British Isles but also across continental Europe, rapidly followed suit, erecting their own stone castles.

Imposing and difficult to capture, stone castles transformed medieval warfare. In fact, sieges of castles became the most common form of military action during the remainder of the medieval era. Furthermore, the evolution of siege weapons and tactics produced a relentless arms race—each new offensive advance was matched by a defensive one, and vice versa. Only when effective cannons appeared in the final medieval years were stone castles rendered obsolete, and this development was one of the principal factors marking the transition from medieval to modern warfare. All of these critical developments were the far-reaching legacy of a single, strong, and innovative military leader who boldly led an army across the English Channel and into the history books.

CHAPTER ONE

Fighting on Foot

Partly because of its size, and also because of its major strategic and political outcomes, the Battle of Hastings was one of the most important military engagements of Europe's medieval period. The start of that long, fateful era coincided with the close of ancient times. Both were marked by one of history's most pivotal events—the collapse of the Roman Empire in the fifth and sixth centuries. Once under way, the medieval age lasted until the rise of Europe's larger modern nations in the 1500s and early 1600s.

The Battle of Hastings was essentially a fight between infantry and cavalry. Harold's Saxon army was made up mostly of foot soldiers who stood stoically in their ranks as the enemy attacked them. That enemy—Duke William's Norman army—was divided into units of both infantry and cavalry. But it was the latter, the mounted warriors, who repeatedly charged the ranks of Saxon infantry, eventually overrunning them and winning the day.

Harold's reliance on his infantry was neither new nor unusual. Foot soldiers, including archers, swordsmen, spearmen, and others, had been the backbone of warfare throughout most of ancient times, and this remained true in medieval Europe's early centuries. William's effective employment of cavalry, however, was part of a larger rise in the importance of mounted warriors in the Middle Ages. In the three centuries that followed the confrontation at Hastings, cavalrymen, often called knights, became a major force in land warfare in Europe.

Yet infantry units neither disappeared nor lost their own military clout in those years. As warfare continued to evolve, generals and other military strategists learned to equip and employ foot soldiers in new and more effective ways. These developments challenged the elite status of cavalry and eventually reinstated the worth, and in some cases the supremacy, of infantry in the medieval era's closing years.

From National Army to Militia

Over the course of the medieval millennium, therefore, the status, use, arms, and tactics of Europe's foot soldiers underwent steady change. One important aspect of this change was in the way local rulers raised and organized their infantry units. Before Rome's demise and the emergence of the first medieval kingdoms, the Roman army dominated military matters in Europe. One reason it was so strong was that it was a national standing army in which soldiers were regularly drafted from the realm's general population. These men underwent intensive training and often gained years of military experience, which made them professional and highly skilled fighters.

In contrast, after Rome's fall the small kingdoms that arose upon its wreckage lacked the strong central government and massive military organization and traditions the Romans had enjoyed. So the post-Roman European kingdoms initially had no national armies. This meant that their rulers had to turn to other means to raise soldiers when they needed them.

The most common solution to this problem in the early medieval centuries was to use the services of a temporary militia. A militia is a part-time military force made up of ordinary citizens. In a military emergency, they grab their own weapons, assemble, take part in a campaign or battle, and then return to their homes.

WORDS IN CONTEXT

militia: Part-time military force made up of ordinary citizens who assemble and fight in an emergency and then return to their homes.

In Saxon England, the militia, or citizen levy, was called the great *Fyrd*. It provided Harold with most of the troops he commanded at Hastings. After William's victory there and the Norman Conquest that followed, the English militia came to be known as the *posse comitatus*, or

The Battle of Hastings (pictured) demonstrated the dominance of mounted soldiers over infantry on the battlefield. Over time military strategists came up with new ways to train and use infantry to create a deadly fighting force.

"force of the county." Each unit was led by a commander called a sheriff. In the early German kingdoms the citizen levy was called the *Heerban* and in Francia (later called France), it was the *arrière-ban*.

From Militia to Standing Armies

In most of these early medieval realms, when a king called up the militia, each manor, or country estate owned by a rich noble, was expected to contribute a certain number of men. That local group of soldiers was called a retinue. With very rare exceptions, the number of infantrymen in a retinue was considerably larger than the number of cavalrymen.

For example, surviving records show that in an English campaign in 1359 the Duke of Lancaster had a retinue that included 90 knights and 423 archers. (Archers were the most common form of foot soldier in

England in this period.) Another nobleman on the campaign, the Earl of Richmond, contributed 35 knights and 200 archers. Later, in the campaign leading to the Battle of Agincourt in 1415, the Earl of Salisbury supplied a retinue of 3 knights and 80 archers to the English army.

The foot soldiers in such retinues usually lived on farms or in small villages located on the estates of wealthy landed nobles. But though the number of soldiers a local lord could raise was frequently impressive, it was nearly impossible to keep them in service for extended periods. Military historian Terence Wise explains: "The length of service in the field owed by these forces varied slightly from country to country but on average was limited to forty days. Service could be extended by paying the troops, although many were reluctant to stay away from their farmlands for long periods and this made it exceedingly difficult to keep an army in the field for any length of time. The peasant levy was under no obligation to serve outside their own country."[6]

Thus, unless a given military campaign was fairly short, a ruler could easily find himself with too few soldiers to achieve success. Another widespread problem with raising infantry locally was that, because these soldiers were rarely professionals, they were often inadequately equipped and lacked proper training. To overcome such shortcomings, it became common to supplement an army's infantry ranks with mercenaries.

In medieval Europe mercenaries were well-armed, well-trained professional fighters who hired themselves out to kings, military generals, or others in need of their services. Some worked alone or in small groups. But many mercenaries formed large bands, often called "free companies." One of the most famous medieval mercenary bands was the White Company, led by Englishman John Hawkwood. Made up of some two thousand archers and a large number of horsemen, the White Company most often worked in Italy, variously fighting for the Italian kingdoms of Florence, Pisa, and Milan.

Over time, these and other European kingdoms grew larger, richer, and better organized. As a result, in late medieval times they took the

> **WORDS IN CONTEXT**
>
> **retinue: Group of soldiers recruited and supported by a wealthy landowner, nobleman, or other powerful individual in medieval Europe.**

crucial step of creating their own permanent national armies in which soldiers had to serve for extended periods of time. A confederation of Swiss city-states in the early 1300s became the first to do so. Some eastern European kingdoms followed suit in the early 1400s, as did France, Hungary, and Germany later in that century.

Infantry Armor and Weapons

The vast majority of medieval infantry—militia, mercenaries, and national forces alike—tended to wear less armor than knights did. The main reason for this was a lack of money. Most foot soldiers could not

WORDS IN CONTEXT

free company:
Medieval
European band
of mercenaries,
or paid soldiers.

afford the extensive array of armor owned by a majority of knights. Nevertheless, some infantrymen used whatever armor they could manage to scrape together, most often comprising a simple mail jerkin, or jacket, called a *byrnie*. Mail, also known as chain mail, consisted of rows of iron rings attached to a leather shirt. Those who could not afford the metal rings made do with the plain jerkin, often reinforced with extra layers of leather. When possible, foot soldiers also wore helmets—typically wide-rimmed iron caps.

The weapons these soldiers wielded varied in type and number from region to region and from one time period to another. But overall the most common during most of the medieval period were swords, knives, spears, axes, maces (clubs), pikes (very long spears), longbows, crossbows, and shields. Many of the lower-class soldiers did not have enough money to purchase newly made weapons. Instead, they rented second- or third-hand or even older weapons from private armories owned by well-to-do individuals. According to historian Andrew Ayton, "A sword might have the most varied 'life story,' passing through many hands, by purchase, bequest [legacy], gift, or seizure, its blade honed or re-hilted according to necessity and taste, perhaps coming to rest finally in a church, a grave, or a river."[7] Some foot soldiers were so poor that they lacked the funds even to rent weapons. Typically, therefore, they resorted to carrying sickles, hoes, and other farm implements into battle.

The Most Common Weapon

Foot soldiers in Europe's medieval era employed a wide variety of weapons, which often varied from one region or time period to another. The most common infantry weapon everywhere in Europe and throughout the era, however, was the sword. This was because swords of that period were highly effective in the hands of almost any fighter with a minimum of training and practical experience. As University of Durham scholar Michael Prestwich says, "Medieval swords were the product of a technology which, with comparatively simple methods, succeeded in producing highly sophisticated weapons." They varied quite a bit in size and function. Some were big, wide, heavy two-handed devices used for hacking and slicing, while others had narrower, pointed blades designed for stabbing bodies and/or piercing armor. "Clearly," Prestwich writes, "there was little point in using a cutting weapon against plate-armor. A powerful thrust might, in contrast, find a weak point and penetrate." Large swords intended for one-handed use became widely popular halfway through the High Middle Ages (in the late 1200s to early 1300s). Yet in the same period smaller swords were fashionable among soldiers in many European countries. One of these was the falchion, a short sword with a wide blade effective for cutting. Whatever specialty a sword was designed for, swords in general, as a class of weapons, were so popular that most soldiers felt naked without one on their person.

Michael Prestwich, *Armies and Warfare in the Middle Ages: The English Experience*. New Haven, CT: Yale University Press, 1996, p. 27.

Of the more commonly used weapons, swords were the most numerous. Usually made of iron, they came in many shapes and sizes, determined by factors such as need, fashion, and personal preference. Maces were less common than swords. The variety of maces employed across Europe was almost dizzying—with heads that could be rounded, knobbed, or spiked, and handles of diverse lengths. Battle axes also varied widely in shape and size.

Slingers, individuals who used leather or cloth slings to hurl rocks, were rarer than they had been in ancient armies but still existed in some parts of medieval Europe. In skilled hands these crude devices were fairly effective up to the length of a modern football field. The rock from a sling could cripple an arm or even kill if it hit a person in the head.

Whatever offensive weapons they used, most medieval infantrymen carried some form of the chief defensive one—the shield. As Christopher Gravett tells it, "Some infantrymen carried a circular wooden shield, often faced and perhaps backed with leather. An iron boss [protruding decoration] riveted to the center of the surface covered a hole through which the hand grasped the shield by an iron strip riveted inside. Many probably had a second strap to secure the forearm, while a third strap allowed the shield to be slung on the back or hung up, as well as preventing it being lost if dropped."[8]

English archers attack a French town with longbows and crossbows during the Hundred Years' War. Archers developed a reputation as a fast and lethal group of fighters.

The Formidable English Longbow

The bow was also employed throughout most of Europe in the Middle Ages. The most common tactic was to begin a battle with one or two volleys of arrows from a few hundred archers, partly to soften up and also to rattle the nerves of an enemy. It has been established, for instance, that Duke William started his assault on the Saxon infantry at the Battle of Hastings with a big discharge of missiles from his bowmen.

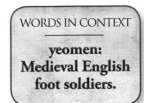

WORDS IN CONTEXT

yeomen:
Medieval English
foot soldiers.

Nowhere else in Europe, however, did archers compare with those who developed in England in the three centuries following the encounter at Hastings. Not all English foot soldiers, called yeomen, were bowmen. But those infantrymen who came to use the longbow were by far the most numerous and most lethal.

Despite its name, the longbow's effectiveness was not based on its size, as it was not much longer than the average hunting bow. Also, the longbow could not fire arrows as far as the typical crossbow could. Two specific factors made the longbow more deadly than the crossbow in the average land battle, one being the rapid rate of fire possible with a longbow. An average longbowman was able to load and fire four or five shafts in the same amount of time it took a crossbowman to let loose just one. A yeomen-archer could fire up to a dozen arrows a minute.

This speediness of firing combined with the second major advantage of the longbow to make English archers among the finest infantrymen of the late Middle Ages. That other advantage consisted of the sheer numbers of longbowmen who fought in a typical battle. As Ayton says, "Massed archery by men able to unleash perhaps a dozen shafts per minute would produce an arrow storm, which at ranges of up to 200 yards [183 m] left men clad in mail and early plate armor, and particularly horses, vulnerable to injury, while causing confusion and loss of order in attacking formations.[9]

One potential danger for these bowmen was that they could be run down and killed by enemy cavalrymen who had managed to get through the initial arrow storm. To lessen this danger, in the early 1400s an English commander came up with a novel idea. Longbowmen were to carry three or four long wooden stakes, sharpened on both ends, into battle along with their bows. After letting loose a volley of arrows, an archer would drive one end of each stake into the ground in front of him, so that the other end pointed outward at an angle. Any oncoming horses would be impaled, or at least badly injured, by these spikes.

Scholar Michael Prestwich points out that this clever defensive arrangement "made it possible for the archers to establish a new defensive position with great speed." Moreover, these infantrymen could pack even more of a punch if necessary. "In addition to their bows and stakes," Prestwich says, "they had axes, mallets, or swords at their belts."[10] With these backup weapons, they often held their own in the hand-to-hand fighting that occurred if and when the enemy managed to penetrate the English lines.

The Widely Feared Swiss

No less fearsome than the English longbow on late medieval European battlefields was another deadly weapon employed by masses of foot soldiers—the pike. Spears roughly 6 to 7 feet (2 m) long had been used by infantry in many parts of Europe all through the early medieval era. But in the 1100s and 1200s, a few local military strategists and commanders saw the wisdom of lengthening the spear and making it more specialized.

The result was the battle pike.

The weapon first appeared in three places—Scotland, Flanders (made up of parts of present-day northern France, Belgium, and the Netherlands), and Switzerland. But the pike reached its greatest length and effectiveness among the Swiss. Their crack late medieval infantry wielded pikes up to 18 feet (5.4 m) long. These soldiers also trained long and hard, including learning how to go on the offensive as the English longbowmen did, rather than merely to assume defensive stances, as had King Harold's foot soldiers at Hastings.

The Swiss pikemen stood together in a large, dense formation often referred to as a hedge. The Swiss called it the *Gewalthaufen*. Standing in about twenty rows, one behind another, its members held their weapons

The Lethal Longbowmen at Crécy

England's enemies often made the mistake of underestimating the abilities and sheer lethality of the English longbowmen. One example of such arrogance that proved disastrous occurred in the first major battle of the Hundred Years' War, fought in 1346 at Crécy, in northern France. Facing the English infantry were masses of heavily armored knights supported by mercenary crossbowmen from the Italian kingdom of Genoa. The Genoese opened the battle with loud war cries designed to frighten the English yeomen. But the latter, unafraid, stood their ground. Then, according to the vivid account by the fourteenth-century French historian Jean Froissart:

> The English archers stepped forth one pace and let fly their arrows so wholly [together] and so thick, that it seemed like snow. When the Genoese felt the arrows piercing through heads arms and breasts, many of them cast down their crossbows and [retreated]. . . . Ever still, the Englishmen shot wherever they saw thickest press [the most men]. The sharp arrows ran into the knights and into their horses, and many fell, horse and men, among the Genoese, and when they were down, they could not get up again, [for] the press was so thick that one overthrew another. And also among the Englishmen there were certain rascals that went afoot with great knives, and they went in among the knights and slew and murdered many as they lay on the ground, both earls, barons, knights, and squires.

Quoted in G.C. Macauly, ed., *The Chronicles of Froissart,* trans. Lord Berners. London: Macmillan, 1904, pp. 104–5.

outward. This produced a massive forest of sharpened pike-points, a powerful and frightening barrier capable of warding off almost any enemy charge. "The first four ranks of pikemen," writes Douglas Miller, an expert on medieval Swiss warfare, leveled their pikes, creating

an impenetrable wall, while the fifth and remaining ranks would hold their weapons upright, ready to fill in any gaps. Because of its length, the pike was held differently by each of the first four

Battle pikes such as these from medieval Europe maimed and killed anyone unfortunate enough to encounter the sharpened end of the weapon. The Swiss perfected the use of pikes, lengthening them and training soldiers in tactics that challenged even their bravest foes.

ranks. The front rank would kneel down with the weapon held low, while the second stooped with the butt held under their right foot. The third rank held the pike at waist level and the fourth rank held it at head height. This classic defensive formation could stop any cavalry charge.[11]

At a commander's order, the *Gewalthaufen* also went on the offensive. The pikemen were so well trained and drilled that they could perform complex maneuvers, including sharp changes of direction, amazingly fast. Moreover, they were supported by units of foot soldiers wielding crossbows and other weapons. Together, the pikemen and their supporters numbered in the tens of thousands, made possible by the creation of a national army in Switzerland in the 1300s. A military draft allowed the Swiss to forge a permanent army of up to fifty-four thousand strong. At the time, other Europeans viewed that number as astounding. These factors explain why the Swiss armies, composed solely of infantry, were the most widely feared and successful military force in medieval Europe's final years.

CHAPTER TWO

Killers on Horseback

If the words *medieval warfare* call to mind any single image in the minds of most people, it is that of the heavily armored knight, who has been widely popularized in modern literature, art, and film. States Andrew Ayton, "For while the armies of the Roman Empire and early modern Europe were dominated by foot soldiers, the corresponding role in those of the Middle Ages was played by men on horseback. The armored knight, mounted on a colorfully caparisoned [decorated] warhorse, is an indelible symbol of medieval Western Europe."[12]

Yet that mounted, armored fighter did not exist at the start of the medieval period. Although there were cavalry units in the early Middle Ages (from the 500s through the 900s CE), their members wore minimal armor, so they are frequently called "light cavalry." Also, in part because of that general lack of effective protection, they rarely, if ever, took part in direct charges against enemy infantry or horsemen, a tactic military experts call shock action. The reality is that it took several centuries for well-armored knights, or "heavy cavalry," to evolve.

Maintaining Cavalry Traditions

That evolution of medieval Europe's elite class of killers on horseback, as some modern observers have called them, had its roots in the Roman Empire. In Roman times, the region now occupied by the nation of France was called Gaul. Beginning in the 300s

CE, a Germanic tribal people known as the Franci, better known as the Franks, settled in Gaul. As time went on the area came to be called Francia after them. (Over subsequent centuries *Francia* became *France*.)

Rome had long kept large horse-breeding estates in Gaul, which had contributed many of the mounts used by cavalry units across the Roman Empire. When that vast realm collapsed in the fifth and sixth centuries, the Franks inherited these estates and maintained them. Partly for this reason, medieval France's first two royal dynasties (ruling families), the Merovingians and Carolingians, had strong cavalry traditions from the outset.

The Merovingians ruled from the late 400s to the 750s, at which time the Carolingians took the throne. Subsequently, the Carolingians held sway in most of France until the late 900s. Both of these lines of rulers recognized a major reason for their maintaining large units of horsemen in warfare: Two of the Franks' most dreaded enemies employed mobile armies made up principally of cavalry. One was the Avars, a fierce tribal people originally hailing from central Asia. The other consisted of Muslim Arabs, who had recently swept across northern Africa and entered and conquered Spain. The Franks realized that they could not effectively counter and defeat these foreign horsemen without maintaining strong cavalries of their own.

WORDS IN CONTEXT

**shock action:
Direct charges by
cavalry on enemy
battle lines.**

By the close of the Carolingian era, these Asian and Muslim intruders had ceased to be a threat to Europe. Even then, however, the Franks and other Europeans who had built up large cavalry units felt it would be unwise to dismantle them. In the words of historian Bernard S. Bachrach, none of Europe's "post-Carolingian states that supported such forces could give them up as long as their potential domestic adversaries [i.e., their neighbors] did not. Without a broad and enforceable general agreement regarding the elimination of [those forces], any government that might undertake partial disarmament on its own would face the risk of placing itself in a disadvantaged position."[13]

As a result, European military cavalry traditions continued, as did the ongoing transformation of these cavalrymen into a class of elite warriors. The forerunners of the classic medieval knight, they came to see themselves as special in part because they tended to be wealthier than infantrymen and other soldiers. Horses were expensive to buy and raise. It was also very costly to equip and train a mounted fighter, so over time many such warriors acquired enhanced social status.

Weapons, Plus a Pivotal Invention

One major reason that the Frankish and other early medieval horsemen did not yet qualify as true, or full-fledged, knights was related to the nature of their armor, weapons, and tactics. The armor worn by Frankish cavalry consisted mostly of mail. It gave the wearer a fair degree of flexibility, including allowing him to mount his horse and use his weapons with more ease than would have been possible wearing heavier, more rigid armor. A serious shortcoming of mail, however, was its lack of full protection. Sword blows that struck it at an angle were often repelled, but a straight-on thrust usually pierced mail shirts.

As did foot soldiers, early European cavalrymen employed swords and spears, and in some cases bows, as well as shields. Trying to maneuver these items effectively without falling off one's steed was difficult enough. So taking part in shock action—which usually entailed using a lance (a long spear with a handle) in a frontal assault on an enemy—was extremely difficult and risky.

A major cause of this limitation was that these light cavalrymen knew nothing of an uncomplicated but crucial invention—the stirrup. As Archer Jones points out, without stirrups, "a rider had to depend on the pressure of his knees to hold himself on his horse. This feeble seat made it awkward for a soldier, especially an unpracticed rider, to fight mounted."[14]

The arrival of the stirrup in western Europe in the eighth or ninth century was therefore a revolutionary advance in the evolution of cavalry warfare in general and the full-fledged knight in particular. First, riders equipped with stirrups were significantly better able to stay seated on their steeds, even when a missed sword stroke threw them off balance. Also, Jones writes, a cavalryman could "increase his height above an opponent on foot

Twelfth-century knights wear both mail and hauberk for protection in battle. These and other improvements in cavalry armor added to the fearsome might of mounted warriors.

26

The Pomp of Horsemen on the March

Medieval poets often described the image of armies on the march, especially their cavalry units. One surviving document of this type chronicles a major military expedition led by England's King Edward I in July 1300. The author, whose identity is uncertain, ably captures the pomp and circumstance of hundreds of knights decked out in shiny plate armor and accompanied by squires or other assistants who displayed richly decorated banners:

> There were many rich caparisons [decorations] embroidered on silks and satins; many a beautiful pennon [flag] fixed to a lance and many a banner displayed. And afar off was the noise heard of the neighing of horses. Mountains and valleys were everywhere covered with sumpter [pack] horses and wagons with provisions, and sacks of tents and pavilions [very large tents]. And the days were long and fine. . . . Then were the banners arranged, when one might observe many a warrior there exercising his horse, and there appeared three thousand brave men-at-arms. Then might be seen gold and silver, and the noblest and best of all rich colors so as to entirely illuminate the valley. [After the tents went up], leaves, herbs, and flowers gathered in the woods were strewed within them. And then our people took up their quarters.

Quoted in N.H. Nicolas, *The Siege of Carlaverock*. London: J.B. Nichols, 1828, pp. 3, 65.

by standing in his stirrups. In addition, this innovation made it possible for mediocre riders to perform well and greatly enhanced the effectiveness of the best heavy cavalry. Thus, the stirrup, so simple in concept, produced one of technology's most fundamental modifications in land warfare."[15]

The adoption of the stirrup made Frankish cavalry units, already superior to other European mounted forces, truly fearsome. A Byzantine military document of the period warned, "So formidable is the charge of the

Frankish cavalry, with their broadsword, lance, and shield, that it is best to decline a pitched battle with them till you have put all the chances on your side." Overall, therefore, "it is easier and less costly to wear out a Frankish army by skirmishes, protracted operations in desolate districts, and the cutting off of supplies, than to attempt to destroy it at a single blow."[16]

Advances in Cavalry Armor

Despite the arrival of the stirrup, which made direct cavalry charges feasible, the Franks and other Europeans who adopted it still avoided shock action when possible. This was partly because cavalry armor still gave riders only minimal protection. So although a charge by horsemen could potentially devastate the front ranks of an enemy's infantry, those foot soldiers could, in turn, badly damage the mounted attackers. As a result, for a while cavalry units were more often used to protect the flanks (sides) of traveling armies, to chase away ambushers, to raid villages, to harass the flanks and backs of enemy troops during a battle, and to pursue fleeing enemy soldiers.

Charges by heavy cavalry composed of knights did, however, eventually become a frightening fact of warfare. This was made possible primarily by a steady series of improvements in cavalry armor during the High Middle Ages, which lasted from about 1000 to 1300. Starting in the eleventh century, when Duke William scored his great victory at Hastings, the mail shirt, now called a hauberk, became longer and heavier. Also, cavalrymen adopted the coif, a mail hood that covered the head. Then came arm and leg protectors, along with gloves made of mail.

WORDS IN CONTEXT

hauberk:
Elongated mail
shirt worn by
both infantry
and cavalry.

The twelfth and thirteenth centuries witnessed still more improvements in cavalry armor. From about 1150, for example, most European knights started using a loose cloth garment—the surcoat (or surcote)—over their mail armor. Later, in the 1200s, according to Ayton,

> iron plate or hardened leather defenses for the elbows, knees, and shins first appeared. And during the following hundred and fifty years, protection for arms and hands, legs, and feet became

steadily more complete. From the mid-to-late thirteenth century, the torso of a well-equipped knight would be protected by a sur-coat of cloth or leather lined with metal plates—a coat of plates, which by the mid-to-late fourteenth century would be supplemented, or wholly replaced by a solid breast-plate.[17]

The late 1300s therefore marked the zenith of this ongoing trend toward the adoption of full suits of plate armor by mounted warriors. These true knights typically provided heavy armor for their horses as well. Calling units of these fighters heavy infantry was completely appropriate, for as Jones explains, "A suit of the new armor could weigh seventy pounds. And, together with its own armor, the horse had to carry over 100 pounds of metal alone. With a horse protected from lance wounds in the chest and the rider virtually proof against [protected from] harm, the knight became far more formidable."[18]

Heavy Cavalry and Other Arms Systems

These increases in the weight and protective qualities of armor quite naturally made some of the weapons wielded by earlier medieval cavalrymen impractical. Because wearing plate armor reduced a rider's flexibility of movement, for instance, he no longer used the bow or spear. His chief weapons instead became the sword and lance. Cavalry swords grew longer and heavier than ever before, and lances ranged from 10 to 12 feet (3 to 3.6 m) in length and featured a flared section in the rear to protect the knight's hands and forearms.

WORDS IN CONTEXT

pommel: On a horse's saddle, an upright knob usually made of wood covered by leather.

Working in tandem with stirrups and advances in armor, the improved lance was a key factor in the emergence of the massive, destructive cavalry charges depicted in modern books and movies. Still another factor that made such tactics possible was the introduction of big, sturdy, wraparound saddles in about 1100. The horseman rested the back of his lance against the saddle's pommel (an upright knob made of wood and leather). This absorbed much of the force caused by the impact of crashing into an enemy line. Modern military historians call this formidable use of lance and saddle the "couched lance technique."

Knights began outfitting their horses in full steel plate armor (pictured) by around 1400. The armor for both the horse and knight could easily weigh more than one hundred pounds.

Military commanders took full advantage of these advances. They were now able to use their units of knights as one of several different arms systems that combined during an attack on an opposing army. Ideally, a commanding general first ordered his archers to soften up the enemy, killing some and tiring the others. Then his knights lowered their lances and charged the opposing lines, shattering them, or at least pushing them back and creating gaps in their ranks. Finally, he sent his own soldiers into those openings, in so doing bringing fresh troops to bear against the exhausted enemy infantry. Meanwhile, that general's heavy cavalry turned around and assaulted the opposing army from the rear. Not every battle progressed in this exact manner. But these were the basic arms systems and tactics that each commanding general took onto the field and used in various ways in hope of gaining the advantage.

WORDS IN CONTEXT

couched lance:
Lance with its
back end resting
against a saddle,
giving the lance
extra power and
stability.

Not surprisingly, the effectiveness of a general's army depended in large degree on how many well-equipped, experienced fighters, particularly knights, he could muster. The number of knights in a given nation or region varied widely. So did the amount of battle experience they had accumulated.

For example, evidence suggests that roughly five thousand knights existed in England at any given time during the century and a half following the fight at Hastings in 1066. But not all of these heavy cavalrymen took part in any single military campaign or battle. The eleventh-century English chronicler Oderic Vitalis reported that a powerful noble named William Rufus was alone able to mobilize some seventeen hundred knights for a military campaign in 1098. At first glance that number may seem small. After all, it represented only about a third of the knights in the kingdom. Yet compared to how many knights took part in each of the campaigns of the period in question, the number that Rufus mustered turns out to be unusually large. Much more typical was the force of five hundred knights that King Henry II took with him on a campaign in Ireland in 1171.

Knightly Conceit and Overconfidence

Even when a military general was able to amass many hundreds of knights for a battle, however, there was no guarantee that he and they would be successful. The opposing army might be considerably bigger, for instance. Or the opposing commander might have a superior strategy.

Another factor that sometimes worked against the effectiveness of large units of heavy cavalry on the battlefield was excessive pride and arrogance. Many medieval European knights viewed themselves as superior

The Perils of Overconfidence

In part because many knights were well-to-do members of the upper classes, they were often arrogant and viewed themselves as superior to foot soldiers, most of whom came from the lower classes. This attitude sometimes caused these elite cavalrymen to become overconfident and make fatal mistakes on the battlefield. A well-known example took place in 1119. France's king Louis VI gathered a small army, which featured about four hundred knights, and entered Normandy (in northwestern France), then under English control. The English monarch Henry I, who had roughly five hundred heavy cavalrymen of his own, met Louis in battle. Henry told four hundred of his knights to dismount and stand behind the other hundred, who remained on their mounts. Thinking that his own horsemen could easily overrun "mere" infantrymen, the French ruler unwisely ordered his knights to charge the English ranks. Although these attackers were able to penetrate Henry's small number of mounted soldiers, the collision of the opposing knights significantly slowed the French riders' momentum. That allowed the many dismounted English knights to surround the French horsemen. They yanked them down from their steeds and either slew or captured them, thereby achieving an overwhelming victory.

to average folk and were notorious for their conceit and overconfidence. Members of Europe's oldest and proudest cavalry establishment, French cavalrymen were particularly susceptible to this sort of thinking. As a result, late medieval France lost several battles because its commanders, often cavalrymen themselves, were guilty of poor judgment.

An example is the Battle of Agincourt in 1415. That year England's king Henry V invaded France, and masses of French knights and other soldiers converged on the intruders, vowing to crush them. The French were certain of victory partly because they outnumbered the English more than two to one. In addition, when the armies faced each other on the battlefield, the French knights saw that a major portion of Henry's forces consisted of infantry, including large numbers of longbowmen. Viewing those archers as socially and militarily inferior to themselves, the French horsemen were confident of success. There was no doubt in their minds that "the English must fall an easy prey to them,"[19] writes Enguerrand de Monstrelet, a French noble of the period.

The events of the subsequent epic military clash swiftly put this brash attitude to rest, however. When the French knights charged, they were devastated by one colossal English arrow storm after another. "Their horses were so severely [wounded] by the archers," Monstrelet recalls, that they galloped wildly, causing great confusion in the French ranks. "Horses and riders were tumbling on the ground and the whole French army was thrown into disorder." Terrified, other French soldiers "fled and this caused so universal a panic in the army that a great part followed the example."[20]

Vanished from the Battlefield

Even though the arrogance of medieval knights sometimes worked against them, more often than not they proved an asset in battle during most of the High Middle Ages. Nevertheless, by the final years of that era, historian Robert Jones points out, their military effectiveness and at times dominance over infantry "had vanished from the battlefield."[21] One reason for this dramatic development was that cavalry armor and weapons became more and more expensive. Eventually, as national governments increasingly switched from militia to standing armies, the costs of maintaining large units of knights became unaffordable.

Another reason for the demise of medieval cavalry was that infantry became increasingly strong in the period's last century and a half. Still another factor was the development of firearms in those same years. Cannonballs and bullets fired by hand-held guns rendered even the heaviest armor useless to those horsemen who were unfortunate enough to be hit by them. Military strategists saw that the wisest approach was to eliminate most of a cavalryman's armor, along with the lance, and give him a gun. In this way, medieval cavalry transitioned into early modern cavalry, and thereafter traditional European knights existed only in history books, novels, and movies.

CHAPTER THREE

Castles Under Siege

"Castles were the unambiguous statements of powerful figures that they were prepared to invest heavily in fortifications to defend their own interests." This is how British historian R.L.C. Jones describes the most important of the many structures erected in medieval Europe. Castles, he continues,

> complicated the way war was waged. With more fortifications in the landscape, the siege began to predominate as the most effective style of warfare. Few campaigns were waged during the period 800–1450 without a siege being laid to at least one, and sometimes several, key strongholds. Only where societies relied less on castles [did] siege warfare remain of secondary importance. Sieges far outnumber pitched battles, naval skirmishes, mounted raids, and all other forms of warfare during the period.[22]

Why Sieges Were Important

For several important reasons, sieges of castles, and at times fortified towns, became the chief form of warfare in medieval times. First, these places dominated politics and most social life. This was especially true during the High Middle Ages (ca. 1000–1300). Castles, located either in the countryside or in towns, were the main residences of the kings, queens, dukes, and other nobles. These fortified habitations were also where monarchs, nobles, and other leaders made the decisions and issued the orders that kept a kingdom running smoothly. Functions such as making laws, dispensing justice, determining tax rates, and overseeing food distribution occurred behind the tall, protective walls of castles and fortified towns. Thus, as tools of political and social control, these places were the natural targets of enemy armies seeking to conquer or disrupt a country.

Castles were also major military objectives in themselves because many of the trained knights and other soldiers in a given region either lived in them or were temporarily stationed in them. These structures were also most frequently the main storehouses of weapons, horses, and other instruments of war. Another crucial military value of castles was their location, which was almost always strategic. As Christopher Gravett says, they "were often situated on roads or rivers and frequently near junctions. Therefore, if an invading body was of inadequate strength, it was forced to give such strongholds a wide berth, leading to major inconvenience and loss of time. In order to secure a conquered country, the castles themselves had to be captured."[23]

The military importance of castles and fortified towns was neither new nor confined to the medieval era. Fortifications and the sieges intended to capture or destroy them were common in both Europe and the Middle East in ancient times. The Assyrians and Persians, centered in what are now Iraq and Iran, and the Greeks and Romans, who long controlled the Mediterranean lands, all created large walled fortresses and towns and developed siege warfare into a genuine art. In fact, the medieval kingdoms that inherited Europe after Rome's disintegration based their knowledge of conducting sieges largely on Roman models.

Also as with ancient sieges, medieval ones had two principal and opposing facets, much like the contrasting sides of a single coin. One facet was offensive in nature. That is, one party sought to attack and take a castle or town. In contrast, the other side of the coin was defensive in nature, as those who dwelled in the castle or town tried to counter the assault and keep the enemy out.

Built to Maintain Security

Hoping to thwart any attack launched against them, the builders of European castles incorporated as many security features as they could into their basic design, including ways to stop besiegers from getting over, under,

Under siege in the 1300s, defending archers try to protect their castle from enemy archers and foot soldiers. With their storehouses of weapons and horses, castles represented attractive targets for attackers.

or through the walls and other defenses. Some of these features became outdated when new tools for waging offensive sieges were invented. The defenders then had to come up with ways to neutralize those new tools. In turn, this stimulated the attackers to try to find still more ways to outsmart the besieged, and so forth. Siege warfare in medieval Europe therefore contained a kind of military arms race related to penetrating fortifications on the one hand and to maintaining their security on the other.

Few castles existed in Europe before the Battle of Hastings and the Norman conquest of England. Afterward, most of the early fortresses were motte and baileys, consisting mainly of small earthen mounds and wooden stockades. Duke William's initial intention in erecting these structures was to use them as guard posts to watch over and control specific regions.

A clear example of the effectiveness of this approach was William's first large motte and bailey, established at Berkhamsted, 25 miles (40 km)

The Greatest Castle of All?

Most of the stone castles erected in Europe in the second half of the Middle Ages were based to one degree or another on the large stone castles built in the Middle East in the ancient and early to mid-medieval periods. Of the latter, the most impressive was the Krak des Chevaliers—often called simply "the Krak" for short—near the Mediterranean coast in western Syria. A leading European military organization, the Knights Hospitaller, used it as a Crusader fortress in the 1100s and 1200s. Able to hold up to two thousand soldiers at a time, the Krak was "arguably the greatest military structure to survive from the Middle Ages," British historian Geoffrey Hindley states. In describing only a few of its many complex defenses, he says that any enemy who managed to break through the gate in the outer defensive wall

> found himself in a covered passage known as the great ramp, heading up a path flanked by loopholes for archers [to fire through], pierced by roof holes for the deposit of missiles and liquid fire [onto attackers' heads], and broken half way along its length by a hairpin bend curved back on itself, which then led to the upper main gate. Attacking from the south meant crossing a moat before scaling a massive wall defended by a sloping [stone ramp]. Should that outer area be breached, the attackers confronted a second water obstacle, the *berquil*, or reservoir, over which loomed three massive towers.

Geoffrey Hindley, *Medieval Sieges and Siegecraft*. New York: Skyhorse, 2009, p. 19.

northwest of London, in the late fall of 1066. Erected in only a few weeks, the castle featured a motte about 40 feet (12 m) high. The bailey was about 500 by 300 feet (150 by 91 m) in extent and surrounded by a tall stockade. At least one water-filled moat ran along the perimeter of the fence.

This imposing structure, garrisoned by several hundred soldiers, was part of William's first major goal following the fight at Hastings. He hoped to persuade the Saxon nobles who then controlled London, and who still opposed him, to surrender the city. Placing the castle beside the key road leading from London northward into the Midlands (south-central England) was meant to send a message to them. William knew that the native Saxons had no large-scale military installations of their own and correctly reasoned that the sudden appearance of such structures would intimidate the locals. As British historian Geoffrey Hindley puts it, the first Norman castles sent "an unmistakable signal to a conquered people to heed the alien oppressor and robber of their liberty."[24] Thus, seeing the new motte and bailey at Berkhamsted, along with other castles rising nearby, the nobles in London realized they were outmatched. They soon surrendered to William without a fight.

It appears that England's new Norman ruler had planned all along to eventually replace most of his motte and baileys with stronger, more permanent stone versions. This advanced castle-building program began in the last decades of the eleventh century and influenced builders across Europe. Archer Jones describes the first Norman stone fortresses, which were fairly small and simple compared to later versions: "The early Norman castle," he writes, "concentrated almost all of its strength in a single enormous tower known as a donjon or keep." This impressive structure "combined height and a maximum space inside with only a narrow perimeter to defend. Defenders needed only men enough to man the battlements and to drop things down on anyone trying to sap [dig beneath] the base of the wall."[25]

WORDS IN CONTEXT

keep: Also called *donjon*, a large stone tower located at or near the center of a medieval castle.

Most of the Norman stone keeps were square in shape. Each had a small square turret—a defensive box or projection—rising upward from the top of each corner. The keep acted either as a secure residence for the owner or a last refuge for the owner and other upper-class residents of the area during an emergency.

Most often a narrow courtyard surrounded the keep. That open space itself was lined by tall defensive walls, often termed curtain walls. Inside these barriers the builders installed workshops, stables, storerooms, and living quarters for the soldiers who manned the defenses. Meanwhile, the outer walls' perimeter was frequently lined with a deep, water-filled moat intended to keep attackers away from the walls. Extra courtyards and sets of defensive walls were added to many of the first stone fortresses in the two centuries that followed, even while much larger and more complex castles were built from scratch.

Breaching the Walls

These defenses were at first adequate to the task of keeping a local lord and his family, supporters, and servants secure from assault. However, attackers rapidly devised ways of getting past the outer walls. One of the earliest was to employ scaling ladders, which were made of wood and tall enough to reach the tops of the battlements. Speed was of the essence in climbing these ladders, as the defenders naturally tried to knock them away as quickly as possible. Usually several besieging bowmen and slingers raked the battlements with covering fire just after the ladders were raised. This was intended to keep the defenders back long enough to allow the climbers to make it to the top without interference.

WORDS IN CONTEXT

sap: In a siege, a tunnel dug beneath a castle wall in hope of giving the besiegers access to the fortress or causing the wall to collapse.

Another method early attackers used to breach a castle's walls was to tunnel beneath them. Unless they were erected atop solid rock, as was the case with only a few castles, the walls were vulnerable to sapping operations. Most often the goal was to get inside the structure by causing sections of its walls to collapse. "Driving a passage through dangerously unstable earth, the sappers used timbers to prop up the roof," historian John Burke explains. "When they reached the target area, the tunnel was packed with branches, brushwood, rags, grease—anything which would burn—and the whole mass set ablaze."[26] The fire destroyed the timbers, causing a cave-in, which in turn brought down the portion of wall above.

Digging such tunnels could be painfully slow, as shown by English monarch King John's siege of Rochester Castle in southeastern England in 1215. The operation took almost seven weeks of grinding labor to complete, while the besieged, consisting of local rebels who opposed the king, managed to hold out against other forms of assault. A writer of the

An aerial view of Arundel Castle in England shows the raised motte and tower, or keep, (center) and two baileys (lower and upper open areas behind the castle walls). Motte and baileys steadily developed from simple earthen mounds and wooden stockades to castles and walls built from stone.

time, known as the Barnwell chronicler, was prompted to exclaim, "Our age has not known a siege so hard-pressed, nor so strongly resisted!"[27] Nevertheless, John's tunnel proved a success in the end, as described by researcher Roy Ingleton. The sap, he says, ran "under the curtain wall to

Women in Sieges and Other Medieval Warfare

Women played many important roles in medieval warfare. They served as nurses, transported supplies, fashioned weapons, and performed other important work that backed up the men who did the actual fighting. In addition, medieval historians recorded instances here and there of women who fought alongside their husbands, fathers, and sons. One prominent example occurred in 1472 at Beauvais, in northern France. That rich market town became the target of a powerful nobleman, Duke Charles of Burgundy, who decided to lay siege to and seize it. But he soon encountered some unexpected and unwanted surprises.

At first, the duke's large siege devices opened up several gaping breaches in some of the town's defensive walls. When his soldiers tried to enter the town through those openings, however, they met with overwhelming resistance by the defenders, who repeatedly hurled them back. The stunned attackers soon reported back to Charles that many of the fighters protecting the breaches were women. Amazingly, they were well trained in the use of swords, bows, and axes. One of those ax-wielding females was Jeanne Laisné, whose heroics earned her the name Jeanne Hachette, or "Jeanne the hatchet-woman." Witnesses saw her slice her way through the Burgundian ranks and seize their banner—then considered a feat of phenomenal strength and bravery, even for a male soldier.

the tower on the southeast corner of the keep, to which the beleaguered [stressed and exhausted] garrison had retreated. John then used the fat of forty pig carcasses to burn through the tunnel's timber supports, causing it to collapse, taking the huge tower above with it.[28]

A Leap Forward for Defenders

As in the Rochester siege, castle defenders did not sit idly by while an enemy was digging a sap. Typically, archers sprayed the areas around a tunnel's front end, hoping to pick off some of the diggers as they entered and exited. The defenders also learned to dig their own tunnels directly below those of the attackers, thereby causing the upper saps to collapse before they reached the walls.

In addition, major improvements in castle design occurred after the start of the First Crusade in 1096. At the urgings of Pope Urban II, thousands of knights and other European soldiers journeyed to what are now Palestine and Israel. Their objective was to free Jerusalem and other local sites that Christians viewed as sacred from the control of Muslim forces. During the expedition, the European fighters saw many Middle Eastern fortresses up close. Thoroughly impressed, they later carried numerous architectural concepts back to their homelands. "The results," historian Frances Gies explains, "were an astonishing leap forward to massive, intricately designed fortresses of solid masonry."[29]

Among these construction ideas that European builders incorporated into new castles was the arrow loop, also called a murderess. It consisted of a vertical rectangular opening in a castle wall through which skilled bowmen could shoot arrows at besiegers outside. These archers were well protected by a clever feature. The outside of a loop was very narrow, so most enemy bowmen were unable to shoot arrows into it. On the inside, however, the loop sharply widened, allowing the defending archers ample room to maneuver and fire.

> **WORDS IN CONTEXT**
>
> **arrow loop:** Also called *murderess,* a narrow vertical opening in a castle's defensive wall, through which archers fired at attackers.

Another potent new design concept was machicolation. It consisted of a stone ledge or shelf that extended slightly outward from the top of the battlements. Usually the shelf was drilled with holes through which defenders dropped boiling oil or rocks onto attackers below.

Also incorporated into new castles was the drawbridge. A wooden platform lying across the moat, it gave the defenders ready access to the front gate during peacetime. Yet the bridge could be pulled upward during a siege, making it extremely difficult for the attackers to reach the gate and employ a battering ram to break through it.

Besiegers' Lethal Tools

These and other improvements in castle defenses made it considerably harder for an enemy force to capture a large stone castle. Still, many medieval European fortresses did fall, mainly because the besiegers had a wide array of lethal military tools at their disposal. The largest, most imposing, and by far most costly was the siege tower. Because it was very expensive and time-consuming to move over long distances, it was nearly always constructed from timber and other materials lying close to the castle. Hindley describes these formidable contraptions, frequently referred to as "belfries," and tells how they carried soldiers up to and over a fortress's walls:

> At their most elaborate, such towers comprised a wooden structure in several tiers, hung with soaked animal hides as protection from fire-arrows and with ladders going up inside the structure to the top platform. There might be a drawbridge, held in the vertical and affording protection to the troops waiting for the assault. As soon as [those soldiers were] assembled, the bridge was swung down [onto the top of the wall] and the troops forced themselves across as best they could. Ideally, before the charge, bowmen in the tower would sweep the enemy wall to clear it of defenders. [Such a tower was] mounted on a wheeled base so that it could be rolled against the enemy fortress on the orders of the commander.[30]

The larger belfries not only made it possible for soldiers to get inside a fortress, they were also capable of causing a huge amount of damage beforehand. A tower often held archers and slingers, along with catapults, all of which propelled deadly missiles over the walls as it approached. A giant siege tower employed against Kenilworth Castle in west-central England in 1266 contained more than two hundred soldiers and eleven catapults.

As a belfry approached a wall during a siege, the defenders sprang into action. Knowing the device was made chiefly of wood and other flammable materials, they shot fire-arrows in hope of burning it down.

Attackers try to breach the walls of a castle during a siege. Once the walls collapsed, there was little the castle's residents could do to protect themselves.

They also unleashed torrents of arrows and rocks on attackers who tried to deposit debris in the moat so that the tower could cross it to get next to the wall.

Besiegers also routinely used artillery engines, machines that fired rocks and other projectiles at or over the walls. An example is the catapults that were sometimes lodged inside the belfries. Much larger catapults were typically arrayed outside a besieged castle to aid in the attack. Another destructive artillery engine employed in many sieges, the ballista, was an oversize crossbow that discharged spears and/or giant arrows.

More deadly still was the trebuchet, which bore numerous nicknames, including "God's stone thrower," "war wolf," and "bad neighbor." The device featured an enormous balance beam divided into a short arm and a long arm. University of California scholar Paul E. Chevedden explains how it worked. "At the end of the longer arm," he says, was a sling for hurling the missile, and at the end of the shorter one pulling ropes were attached, or, in later versions, a counterweight. To launch a projectile, the short arm, positioned aloft, was pulled downward by traction or gravity or by a combination of both forces. The impetus applied to the beam propelled the throwing arm of the machine upward and caused the missile to be hurled from the sling.[31]

Trebuchets, which came in a variety of sizes, possessed remarkable power. A large one could fling a projectile weighing 220 pounds (100 kg) more than 1,300 feet (400 m)—about a quarter of a mile. One eyewitness account by an English priest describes its use in the siege of Acre (in what is now Israel) by a Crusader army: "It shot with such force, and its blows were so effective, that no material or substance could withstand the unbearable impact without damage, no matter how solid or well-built it was."[32]

Not to be outdone, the defenders of some castles countered the use of such artillery by installing their own artillery inside or atop the walls. In fact, it became customary to hurl the same rocks an enemy had thrown right back at him. And so it went. As each new destructive device or idea incited the invention of an equally hurtful countermeasure, medieval siege warfare's relentless arms race plodded on and on.

WORDS IN CONTEXT

trebuchet: Type of medieval siege artillery that hurled large projectiles by utilizing a sling, wooden balance beam, and counterweight.

CHAPTER FOUR

Assaults by Sea

Compared with medieval warships and navies, modern ones are obviously superior on all counts. The vessels employed in warfare in the Middle Ages were small and difficult to maneuver. They were also incapable of navigating reliably when out of sight of land, so "battles in the open sea were a near-impossibility," Michael Prestwich points out. "When fleets did engage, it was normally in a harbor, or close in-shore. The concept of 'control of the sea' is one that is hard to apply to the medieval period. Ships could not remain at sea for lengthy periods, and were too much at the mercy of tides and winds to exercise really effective control."[33]

Yet despite these many drawbacks of medieval ships, the role they played in warfare was at the least significant and sometimes vital. Whatever the individual physical limitations of these vessels, they could travel faster than any land army. This made them extremely valuable for transporting soldiers and all the horses, weapons, and food they required along either rivers or the coastlines of the Mediterranean, North, and Baltic Seas and Atlantic Ocean. By building a fleet of ships, therefore, a European nation could rapidly bring a large, well-supplied army to bear against most national enemies. Oxford University scholar Felipe Fernandez-Armesto says, "European naval superiority enabled military expeditions to operate successfully, far from home, against adversaries better endowed in every other kind of resource."[34]

Forms of Naval Warfare

Those operations of medieval naval forces took a number of forms. The most common employed ships as transport vehicles to convey soldiers, weapons, horses, food supplies, siege devices, and other basic tools of warfare. Moving these things overland was far more costly and time-consuming. A small fleet of cargo ships could deliver the needed materials to a selected point near or even behind an enemy's lines, in some cases before that enemy was organized and ready to fight. Naval forces were also useful for carrying reinforcements to the battlefront or moving soldiers out of harm's way when a retreat was necessary.

In addition, seagoing vessels were frequently very effective in direct assaults on enemy coasts. This was partly because their speed allowed them to appear suddenly, seemingly out of nowhere, which gave the soldiers they carried the element of surprise. In some cases these soldiers came ashore and marched inland as part of a large military campaign.

At other times such fighters were raiders who attacked and looted a farm, village, or monastery and then quickly sailed away before local military forces could reach the area. This tactic was used to great advantage by the Vikings, Scandinavian marauders who plundered the coasts of northern Europe in the eighth and ninth centuries. Archer Jones describes why they were so successful:

> Talented sailors, the Vikings came in small undecked vessels, usually with a single large sail, but these ships relied primarily on the oars of their crew of forty to 100 fighting men. The profits were so great that these raids became the principal occupation of the Viking communities. Their command of the sea and their ability to beach their boats gave the Vikings wide latitude in their choice of landing places. Therefore, they had unequaled facility [ability] for avoiding their opponents' strengths and concentrating against weakness, readily implementing their raiding strategy and search for weakly defended booty.[35]

Still another form of naval warfare in the medieval era was the larger and more formal naval battle. Such events were strategically important, as shown by the Battle of Sluys, fought near the coast of Flanders (now Belgium) in 1340. The opening salvo of the horrific Hundred Years' War, which pitted England against France, it produced an English victory

Goods are loaded onto a medieval ship. Navies of the period relied on ships for transporting soldiers, weapons, food, and other supplies—a less costly and time-consuming option than going overland.

that kept France from invading southern England. A similar historic naval battle fought in the English Channel in 1588 witnessed an English fleet defeating the mighty Spanish Armada. That victory, won during the reign of England's renowned "warrior queen," Elizabeth I, prevented some fifty-five thousand Spanish fighters, an enormous army in that era, from seizing southern England.

Such large-scale naval battles were fairly uncommon throughout the Middle Ages, however. This was largely because constructing and maintaining large fleets of vessels designed for warfare was simply too expensive for most of the city-states and kingdoms of the period. With few exceptions, a medieval state's war fleet consisted of fewer than fifty craft. That number is tiny compared to the vast navies assembled by ancient Rome and Carthage and modern industrial nations like the United States, Germany, Japan, and Russia.

Early Medieval Warships

The limited number of ships that medieval kingdoms and peoples were capable of amassing was particularly evident in the years directly following the Roman Empire's demise. Moreover, the vessels of that period lacked the speed, storage capacity, and overall military effectiveness of those in the later Middle Ages. The earlier ones were galleys much like those employed by the Greeks, Romans, Phoenicians, and other ancient Mediterranean peoples. They operated primarily by the power of men pulling long oars. The single, small, square-shaped sail that such a ship carried could sometimes supplement the rowers. But it was incapable of powering the vessel for very long in most situations.

WORDS IN CONTEXT

galley: Common in both ancient and medieval times, a wooden ship powered primarily by oars.

A typical early medieval galley was about 100 feet (30 m) long and featured twenty-five oars on each side. In naval terminology, those oars are more often called "benches" in reference to the wooden seats on which the rowers sat. With one man to a bench, there were therefore fifty rowers. Some of the early galleys had two banks of benches, one situated above the other, in which case there were one hundred rowers. Such a vessel also had a few sailors to maintain and guide it and a small number of marines (naval fighters). The rowers were expected to fight alongside the marines during a clash with an enemy.

Because these ships were relatively small yet carried quite a few people, there was no room for large stores of food and other supplies. This meant that they could not remain at sea for more than a few days at a time. For this reason, as well as the lack of effective navigation instruments, galleys usually stayed within sight of coastlines and made frequent stops.

Closely related in many ways to the early Mediterranean galleys, although smaller, were the oared boats that plied the waters of the North

The Battle of Svölder: King Olaf's Demise

Only a few medieval European sea battles were described in any detail by chroniclers of that age. Among them is the battle of Svölder, which took place in the Baltic Sea around the year 1000. One of the opposing navies was commanded by Norway's king, Olaf Trygvason. The other was made up of vessels from Denmark and Sweden, which were allied against Norway. This account of the climax of the battle is from *King Olaf Trygvason's Saga*, part of a larger work by the Icelandic historian Snorri Sturluson. "The fight became hot indeed," Sturluson says, as the Danes and Swedes boarded Olaf's flagship, the *Serpent*.

> So many men of the *Serpent* had fallen that the ship's sides were in many places quite bare of defenders. And [Olaf's enemies] poured in all around into the vessel, and all the [Norwegian] men who were still able to defend the ship crowded aft to the king, and arrayed themselves for his defense. [A witness said that] the gallant few of Olaf's crew [took] refuge on the quarter-deck. Around the king they [stood] in [a] ring. Their shields enclosed the king from foes, and the few who still remained [fought] madly, but in vain. . . . Few were the people left in the *Serpent* for defense against so great a force, and in a short time most of the *Serpent*'s men fell, brave and stout though they were.

Snorri Sturluson, *King Olaf Trygvason's Saga*, in the Project Gutenberg version of the *Heimskringla*. www.gutenberg.org.

Sea. Chief among these were Viking longships. One that was unearthed in modern times—called the Gokstad ship—appears to be typical of the average longship in most ways. It is 76 feet (23 m) long and has sixteen benches to a side, which means it had thirty-two oarsmen. Partly because the Normans were descendents of Vikings who had settled in France, the oared vessels that Duke William built to carry his army across the English Channel in 1066 were very similar to longships.

Late Medieval Warships

Galleys continued to be widely used in the Mediterranean in the second half of the Middle Ages. Some of them were slightly larger than the earlier versions, as shown by studies of the handful of these vessels that archaeologists have found partially intact. Noteworthy was a galley constructed for England's King Henry V, the remains of which were found in an English river in 1933. In its prime, the ship was 125 feet (38 m) long and 50 feet (15 m) wide at the beam (midpoint of its length).

The mighty Spanish Armada (pictured) was outmaneuvered and defeated by an English fleet of ships in 1588. The victory prevented thousands of Spanish fighters from seizing southern England.

The final medieval centuries were also notable for ship designers' introduction of several crucial technical advances. One, which came in the early 1400s, was the addition of a second mast bearing one or two extra sails. Another new mast, the bowsprit, projecting forward from the bow (front) of the ship, added still more sails, increasing the vessel's propulsive power as well as its speed. These developments rapidly eliminated the need for oars.

WORDS IN CONTEXT

roundship: In late medieval and early modern times, a sailing ship with a wider, higher hull than that of a galley.

The result was the emergence of true sailing ships, often called roundships. They had higher, wider hulls than galleys, making them more robust and stable. The extra height was most pronounced in the stern (rear), which featured a so-called "castle," a big cabin, or cluster of small ones, topped by a deck that towered over the rest of the ship. The castle offered a strategic military advantage because archers, slingers, and even small onboard catapults could be stationed there. Its added height increased the chances that their missiles would strike nearby enemy ships.

Sea Fights Like Land Battles

Thanks to these and other advances, warships in the Late Middle Ages grew larger and faster. They also carried more fighters. One critical factor that did not change much until almost the end of the medieval era was the nature of the tactics used in naval warfare. In general, warships and their captains and crews conducted sea battles more or less like land battles.

For example, in the same way that bowmen typically initiated land battles with big volleys of arrows, archers aboard a warship were usually the first to fire on an approaching enemy vessel. If a ship had slingers and spearmen aboard, they fired next. Then, when the two craft got close enough, crewmen on one or both of them hurled a grappling hook with a length of rope attached. When the hook caught hold of an object on the enemy vessel, several men tugged hard on the rope, pulling that vessel alongside their own.

With the two boats locked together, essentially forming a single floating platform, the opposing crews fought it out hand-to-hand, as soldiers did in land battles. In fact, at times three, four, or more ships became locked together, creating an even wider surface for the crews to fight on. Thus, summarizes English scholar Ian Heath, "the main naval tactic was simply to row against an enemy ship, grapple and board it, and clear it with hand weapons before moving on to another vessel."[36]

Medieval Naval Tactics Rendered Obsolete

Eventually, however, as sails steadily replaced oars as the chief means of propulsion, naval commanders saw that they could use those sails to great advantage. They found that the sails' wind-catching capabilities could provide not only power but also increased maneuverability. Moreover, that ability to outmaneuver an enemy could be combined with an extremely deadly weapon—the cannon—which began to be used on ships in the early 1500s.

WORDS IN CONTEXT

man-of-war: English term for a warship featuring sails and cannons.

Thereby, a new set of naval tactics was born. It deemphasized approaching an enemy and engaging in hand-to-hand combat and instead stressed the concept of destroying an opponent from a distance. The cannons, in naval jargon, "guns," that made this possible were mounted in rows below a warship's main deck. Packing the firepower of twenty, thirty, or more guns, a single large sailing ship was now a military threat of immense proportions. From the late 1500s on, the English called such a vessel a *man-of-war*.

With favorable wind conditions and a skilled captain, a man-of-war could easily cripple or sink an entire small fleet of old-style galleys. In a sea battle, a man-of-war's captain focused on maneuvering his ship into a position from which his guns could do the most damage. More often than not, that position was broadside-to-broadside, or parallel. Ideally, the captain's vessel crept up on the enemy ship from the rear, and as it passed by, its guns opened fire, raking the opponent's hull, masts, and rigging.

A Spanish Officer Describes the Armada's Demise

On October 4, 1589, a Spanish naval officer named Francisco de Cuellar wrote a letter to a fellow Spaniard, describing some of the horrors he had witnessed during the enormous battle in which the English defeated the Spanish Armada. In the letter, Cuellar also states that he had washed ashore wearing only his shirt before being rescued by some of his countrymen.

Many were drowning within the ships; others, casting themselves into the water, sank to the bottom without returning to the surface; others on rafts and barrels, and gentlemen on pieces of timber; others cried aloud in the ships, calling upon God; While I was regarding this solemn scene, I did not know what to do, nor what means to adopt, as I did not know how to swim, and the waves and storm were very great; and, on the other hand, the land and the shore were full of enemies [the English], who went about jumping and dancing with delight at our misfortunes; and when any one of our people reached the beach, two hundred savages and other enemies fell upon him and stripped him of what he had on until he was left in his naked skin.

"Captain Cuellar's Account of the Spanish Armada." http://9th-grade-world-history.moscow .groupfusion.net.

The first large-scale test of this new approach to naval warfare was the clash between the English and Spanish fleets in the English Channel in 1588. Spain's king Philip II was intent on capturing and ruling England. So he sent some 130 warships—the infamous Spanish Armada—into the channel to destroy the English fleet, which he expected would clear the way for the invasion.

A packed ship departs for the Crusades. Medieval ships were fairly small and often crowded a lot of people on board. With little room for food and supplies, they could not remain at sea for more than a few days at a time.

The Spanish ships, commanded by the Duke of Medina-Sidonia, were very large, had tall castles, and carried only a few guns. With a military emphasis placed instead on brute manpower, they were crammed with infantrymen—a total of more than eighteen thousand in the fleet. Philip and Medina-Sidonia had planned on using these foot soldiers in a traditional medieval sea fight, in which they would board and capture the smaller English ships one by one.

The English commander, Baron Howard of Effingham, was well aware of the Spanish strategy and proceeded to counter it by employing the relatively new man-of-war tactics. He outfitted his vessels with about two thousand guns, most having a longer range of fire than those of the Spanish. As the battle commenced, his ships sailed circles around the slow-moving Spanish giants, discharging enormous volleys of cannon fire as they went. This continued for many days, and thousands of men went to watery graves. In the end, the armada was defeated, England was saved, and although no one likely realized it at the time, in amazingly short order medieval naval tactics were rendered obsolete.

CHAPTER FIVE

Firearms Revolutionize War

"Gunpowder changed warfare, and in so doing it changed the world,"[37] states historian Thomas F. Arnold. Nonetheless, the invention of gunpowder weapons and their introduction to the battlefield did not revolutionize warfare overnight—in fact, this process took a few centuries. One reason for this slow change is that for many years gunpowder was hard to find. Moreover, its early formulas did not deliver much explosive power. In addition, the first generations of cannons and hand-held guns were crude, overly heavy and bulky, and not very mobile.

Steadily, however, inventors and military engineers eliminated these drawbacks, thereby making firearms immensely more effective. The ultimate result was nothing less than world-altering. It became clear to all that gunpowder weapons "were simply too powerful for ancestral ways of war based on horses and lances, castles and catapults,"[38] in Arnold's words.

At the same time, as the old ways of war were discarded, political and social customs based on building, maintaining, and capturing castles and fortified towns changed, too. Individuals and societies with the most power and influence were no longer those with the strongest walls and finest cavalry. Rather they were the ones best able to harness, exploit, and, most important, consistently improve the technology of firearms. Arnold offers what he calls a "classic opening scene" for this historic military transformation: "A grimy-faced bombardier [gunner] bends over his big-bellied cannon poised to send a great stone ball smashing into a centuries-old castle, an elegant confection of pointy towers and steeply pitched roofs. With that ball, we understand, this gunner is knocking down a way of life—a way of power—as well as reducing a gothic charm to a pile of splintered masonry."[39]

Chinese Contributions

Although the technology of firearms and the use of those weapons in warfare were perfected largely in late medieval Europe, the Europeans did not invent the key to these advances—gunpowder. Exactly where and when this fateful material originated is still uncertain. Yet modern experts feel there is sufficient evidence to zero in on somewhere in China as the where and sometime in the 800s CE as the when. Within that time frame, an unknown individual stumbled on the fact that combining sulfur, charcoal, and potassium nitrate (saltpeter) and exposing the mixture to a flame produced a sudden flash or small explosion.

It appears this newly invented substance—gunpowder—was first used to produce firecrackers, employed then as they are today in celebrations. The Chinese also found gunpowder could be used effectively on the battlefield. They created small rockets that shot upward and exploded in the air, frightening enemies who were unfamiliar with them. In addition, descending rockets sometimes set the roofs of houses on fire. Another military application was a bamboo tube that discharged a burst of fire and smoke when someone touched a flame to some gunpowder packed inside.

The Chinese also developed grenade-like weapons, the general name of which translates roughly as "thunderclap bombs." When they exploded, they apparently generated a flash of light and a very loud noise, which scared enemy soldiers and horses. A twelfth-century Chinese commander named Li Kang recalls in a political memoir, "At night the thunderclap bombs were used, hitting the lines of the enemy well, and throwing them into great confusion. Many fled, howling with fright."[40] There is no evidence, however, that any of these early Chinese gunpowder devices produced explosions powerful enough to destroy units of soldiers or stone walls.

Early European Gunpowder Experiments

That level of firearm technology did not occur in Europe until a century or two later. Fundamental knowledge of gunpowder and its potential for use in warfare passed slowly but steadily from China to Europe during the 1100s and early 1200s. One pathway seems to have been verbal accounts by merchants and other travelers who periodically made the long trek over the handful of trade routes linking the two regions. Some evidence also suggests that a few eastern Europeans witnessed the Mongols, a tribal people who conquered China, using gunpowder weapons.

Hearing about these devices, European inventors became fascinated and started to experiment. They found that the main ingredients of gunpowder could be combined in numerous proportions, and it took a while to find the most effective ones. The famous English scientist Roger Bacon hit on a moderately useful formula in 1267. It mixed the components in fractions of about 29 percent sulfur, 41 percent potassium nitrate, and close to 30 percent charcoal. Bacon found that this combination generated a flash of light and a loud bang, but its detonation produced almost no damage.

Only after several more decades did European inventors begin to find a handful of gunpowder recipes that produced considerable destructive force. Some came fairly close to the modern formula. Meanwhile, by the early 1300s European military engineers had begun to experiment with delivery systems for the gunpowder explosions—that is, the actual firearms. The first examples were not guns but rather grenade-like devices similar to the Chinese thunderclap bombs, only more destructive.

Some of these weapons were relatively small and hand-held, which allowed soldiers to throw or catapult them into enemy camps, castles, or towns. Another version was the first land mine, a big pot of gunpowder that was inserted into a sap dug beneath a castle wall during a siege. Its explosion directly under a wall could help bring that wall down. Conversely, defenders could use the same device to destroy a sap before it reached a wall.

Still another early bomb was the petard (meaning "little fart" in French). It was a large metal container of gunpowder that a soldier hung on the front gate of a castle or fortified town. After lighting the fuse, he ran for cover, hoping the bomb would not ignite before it was supposed to. If it did, and he suffered injury or death, it was said that he was "hoisted [lifted into the air] by his own petard." That phrase is still used today to denote a person whose scheme somehow backfires.

Rudimentary Cannons

Primitive grenades, land mines, and petards remained in use through the remaining years of the medieval period. But it was not long after they appeared that military leaders started complaining that they lacked enough destructive power. So they poured more and more money and resources into making gunpowder weapons more potent. As time went on, Arnold explains, one development was that "gunpowder became cheaper, as its

English scientist Roger Bacon experiments in his laboratory with gunpowder. Bacon discovered a combination of the ingredients that generated a flash of light and a loud bang but did little damage at detonation.

A Noise Like Thunder

After the Chinese discovered gunpowder, they experimented widely with ways to use it in warfare. The so-called thunderclap bomb was one of many results. It was a grenade-like device that made an extremely loud noise when it exploded. One variant of it apparently did more than frighten and confuse enemies on the battlefield. Someone learned to add lime to the powder to blind the enemy as well. In 1161, for example, a military commander, Yu Yun-Wen, achieved a major victory in a battle fought in a river by using trebuchets to deliver his bombs. An eyewitness reported,

> All of a sudden a thunderclap bomb was let off. It was made from [thick] paper and filled with lime and sulfur. Launched from trebuchets, these thunderclap bombs came dropping down from the air and upon meeting the water exploded with a noise like thunder. The sulfur bursting into flames. The paper case rebounded and broke, scattering the lime to form a smoky fog, which blinded the eyes of men and horses so that they could see nothing. Our ships then went forward to attack theirs, and their men and horses were all drowned, so that they were utterly defeated.

Quoted in Joseph Needham, *Science and Civilization in China: Military Technology*. New York: Cambridge University Press, 1986, p. 166.

makers puzzled out better ways of extracting and purifying its chemical components." Furthermore, "corned powder, made by wetting the mixture during manufacture, and drying it in lumps or granules, was both more sharply combustible and more resistant to moisture and separation, and thus degradation over time and during transport."[41]

Even as this research progressed, military experts introduced the earliest cannons, which were initially intended for siege warfare. Rudimentary versions may have first emerged in Europe as early as 1320. But the first certain reference to such weapons is a 1326 order for the manufacture of a few, along with iron balls for them, by the city council of Florence in central Italy. Around that same year, the first known artistic depiction of a cannon appeared in a manuscript by English scholar Walter de Milamete. The weapon, called a *pot-de-fer*, or "iron pot," looked like a bulbous flower vase lying on its side. The illustration shows a soldier lighting its fuse.

WORDS IN CONTEXT

pot-de-fer: Early bronze or iron cannon shaped similarly to a flower vase.

These elementary cannons were not very reliable, in part because the metals used to make them were either too soft or cast too thinly. So when fired they cracked fairly often. The stone and metal missiles they shot, which appropriately came to be called *shot*, were both inaccurate and limited in their range (the distance the shot traveled). As a result, their destructive power was relatively small, and they killed few people. The first known fatality caused by an early European cannon occurred at the English siege of the French town of Orléans in 1428. The victim, Thomas Montacute, Earl of Salisbury, was hit, probably by a lucky shot, while standing above the city gates. "Half his face was blown away,"[42] according to witnesses. Yet he lived on for six agonizing days before dying of blood loss and a raging infection.

An Unprecedented Bombardment

Because cannon technology swiftly progressed, however, these devices steadily became more powerful, reliable, and accurate. One particularly crucial advance took place in about 1370 when engineers began employing several long, thick pieces of iron placed edge to edge and held together by sturdy iron rings. This allowed for the creation of much bigger cannons than ever before.

By the close of that century, all large cannons were termed bombards (the source of the modern term *bombardment*). These monster guns, as some later writers called them, bore pet names and fired balls of enormous weight. According to Geoffrey Hindley,

> "Mons Meg," now in Edinburgh [Scotland], fired a stone shot weighing about 550 pounds. "Dulle Griet," or the "Great Bombard of Ghent [Belgium]," fired one of over 750 pounds. And the "Pumhart von Steyr," ("the bombard of Styria"), in Vienna [Austria], fired a mammoth shot of 1,530 pounds. Given that the explosive force of gunpowder was still relatively weak, such weapons made sense, for that powder was now easily available in quantity and cheap.[43]

With the size of the cannons and their shot now making up for their limited explosive force, it became possible to demolish castle walls. It took a mere two days, for example, for a German prince's big guns to destroy a castle during a siege in 1414. A growing number of fortresses across Europe met a similar fate in the decades that followed. The biggest shock of all to numerous Europeans came in the pivotal year 1453, when the Ottoman Turks used their large cannons to devastate the huge and supposedly invincible walls protecting the great Christian city of Constantinople (now Istanbul, Turkey). Historian John Julius Norwich calls it "a bombardment unprecedented in the history of siege warfare."[44]

WORDS IN CONTEXT

bombard:
General name
of a class of very
large medieval
cannons made
mostly in the
fourteenth
and fifteenth
centuries.

A Landmark Military Campaign

The bombards undoubtedly did a great deal of damage. Yet they had a serious shortcoming that made their use in warfare extremely difficult and expensive—their enormous weight made them almost immobile. Moving a single one overland to a target required many dozens, and sometimes hundreds, of horses and men and a great deal of time; so much time that such a gun could not keep up with the march of the army of which it was a part.

Bombards on fixed and rolling carriages (pictured) were mainly used to fire heavy metal balls at castle walls. The damage of impact could be substantial.

Clearly, military experts and leaders realized, it was imperative to overcome this weight problem. For cannons to become truly useful instruments of warfare, military historian John Keegan states, "they had to be lightened enough to be transported on wheels at the same speed as the army that accompanied them." That way, "foot, horse, and guns could move as an integrated unit within enemy territory."[45]

As it turned out, the rapid pace of improvements in military technology solved this problem in short order. By the late 1400s, a considerably smaller and more mobile cannon—most commonly called a culverin—was coming into general use. Its iron tube, which was more slender than that of a bombard, was cast in a single piece, providing it with tremendous strength and structural integrity. Yet it was also lightweight enough to fit on a modest-size two-wheeled carriage that required only nine or even fewer horses to pull. This not only allowed the weapon to be transported to the site of a siege much faster, it also made cannons practical for use on the open battlefield, where their ability to be moved around fairly quickly was vital.

The remarkable efficiency and military value of the culverin was demonstrated in one of the landmark military campaigns of the late Middle Ages. In the winter of 1493–1494, France's King Charles VIII

Mobility Leads to Enduring Success

The giant cannons that appeared in Europe in the late 1300s and early 1400s were capable of causing considerable destruction. But they were too heavy, difficult, and costly to move to be consistently useful in warfare. The mobility of culverins and other lighter-weight cannons made them much more effective in siege warfare, as well as on the battlefield. One key factor in the success of these smaller cannons was the manner in which they were made. "Because the tubes were cast in one piece," military historian John Keegan explains, "trunnions, short flanges [knobs] projecting just forward of the point of balance, could be incorporated into them, by which [the cannons] could be hung in wooden two-wheeled carriages. The cannon thus became as maneuverable as a small cart." The carriage lent the weapon flexibility and ease of use in another way as well. Namely, manufacturers learned to fashion such a carriage to allow the cannon's barrel "to be depressed or elevated by the manipulation of wedges under the breech [the section just behind the barrel]." Thanks to these and other new developments in cannon mobility, Keegan adds, the artillery revolution of the late Middle Ages "proved enduring. The new guns achieved an effect after which siege engineers had striven for millennia without success."

John Keegan, *A History of Warfare*. New York: Random House, 1994, pp. 321–22.

ordered the production of forty-four state-of-the-art, highly mobile culverins. Adding them to a force numbering around thirty thousand men, in October 1494 he marched into northern Italy and surrounded the castle guarding the town of Fivizzano. Though this fortress had withstood several sieges lasting weeks or months in the past, Charles's cannons blasted huge breaches in its walls in less than a day. News of this extraordinary event traveled speedily and had just the effect that Charles had hoped for. Nearly all the nearby Italian city-states wasted no time in surrendering to him without a fight.

Guns That Soldiers Could Carry

Lightweight cannons were not the only firearms employed by the soldiers in Charles's invasion force. Possibly as many as one in ten of them carried portable, hand-held guns most commonly referred to as *arquebuses*. Extremely little is known about their early development. But most modern scholars think they evolved alongside cannons, starting in the early 1300s.

The first versions of hand-held firearms were made from brass or bronze, measured 8 to 12 feet (2.4 to 3.6 m) in length, and were very heavy and awkward to use. To fire these weapons, gunners had to rest them on standing poles. A soldier inserted some gunpowder into the front of the barrel, followed by a stick to push the powder down tightly. Next, he slipped in the shot, most often a small lead ball. Finally, he stuck a red-hot metal wire into a little hole in the back of the barrel, thereby igniting the powder and firing the weapon. Around 1400, a piece of burning rope called a "match" replaced the wire.

WORDS IN CONTEXT

culverin: **General term for several different lightweight cannons that appeared in Europe in the 1400s.**

In the course of the following two centuries, these primitive guns underwent a steady series of advances. They became shorter and much more lightweight, so a gunner was able to fire one without the aid of a pole. The so-called matchlock mechanism was added in the mid-1400s. It consisted of a smoldering match held in place by a metal lever on the top of the barrel. Pulling the trigger caused a spring to snap and touch a bit of gunpowder in a small pan. The resulting flash made a larger quantity of powder inside the barrel explode, thereby firing the gun.

A late fifteenth-century woodcut depicts armored soldiers firing matchlock guns, or arquebuses. As use of these guns expanded, traditional weapons such as crossbows, spears, and slings gradually became obsolete.

By the late 1400s a long, slim, lightweight version of the weapon, the arquebus—the ancestor of the musket—was widely employed by foot soldiers across Europe. At that time such hand-held guns were already rapidly replacing crossbows, spears, and slings, just as cannons were steadily making catapults and other traditional artillery obsolete. The complete transition from old-fashioned weapons to firearms in warfare was destined to last another couple of centuries. But when the medieval era gave way to early modern times circa 1500 or so, the face of battle had already been mightily transformed. It had changed in ways that early medieval Europeans, and even the later, farsighted military leader Duke William, the victor of Hastings, could never have foreseen.

SOURCE NOTES

Introduction: Medieval Warfare Transformed

1. Quoted in Christopher Gravett, *Hastings 1066: The Fall of Saxon England*. Oxford: Osprey, 1999, p. 64.
2. Gravett, *Hastings 1066: The Fall of Saxon England*, p. 67.
3. Quoted in Charles Oman, *A History of the Art of War in the Middle Ages*, vol. 1. London: Acheron, 2012, p. 164.
4. Quoted in Stephen J. Murray, "From Dot to Domesday: The Battle of Hastings." www.dot-domesday.me.uk.
5. Archer Jones, *The Art of War in the Western World*. New York: Oxford University Press, 1987, p. 113.

Chapter One: Fighting on Foot

6. Terence Wise, *Medieval European Armies*. Oxford: Osprey, 2000, pp. 4–5.
7. Andrew Ayton, "Arms, Armor, and Horses," in *Medieval Warfare: A History*, ed. Maurice Keen. New York: Oxford University Press, 1999, p. 202.
8. Gravett, *Hastings 1066: The Fall of Saxon England*, p. 22.
9. Ayton, "Arms, Armor, and Horses," pp. 203–4.
10. Michael Prestwich, *Armies and Warfare in the Middle Ages: The English Experience*. New Haven, CT: Yale University Press, 1996, p. 136.
11. Douglas Miller, *The Swiss at War, 1300–1500*. Oxford: Osprey, 1999, pp. 13, 15.

Chapter Two: Killers on Horseback

12. Ayton, "Arms, Armor, and Horses," p. 186.
13. Bernard S. Bachrach, "Early Medieval Europe," in *War and Society in the Ancient and Medieval Worlds*, ed. Kurt Raaf-

laub and Nathan Rosenstein. Cambridge, MA: Harvard University Press, 1999, p. 294.

14. Jones, *The Art of War in the Western World*, p. 9.
15. Jones, *The Art of War in the Western World*, p. 103.
16. Quoted in Oman, *A History of the Art of War in the Middle Ages*, vol. 1, pp. 204–5.
17. Ayton, "Arms, Armor, and Horses," p. 200.
18. Jones, *The Art of War in the Western World*, pp. 151–52.
19. Quoted in Society for Medieval Military History, "The Battle of Agincourt, 1415." www.deremilitari.org.
20. Quoted in Society for Medieval Military History, "The Battle of Agincourt, 1415."
21. Robert Jones, *Knight: The Warrior and World of Chivalry*. Oxford: Osprey, 2011, p. 212.

Chapter Three: Castles Under Siege

22. R.L.C. Jones, "Fortifications and Sieges in Western Europe, ca. 800–1450," in Keen, *Medieval Warfare: A History*, pp. 163–64.
23. Christopher Gravett, *Medieval Siege Warfare*. Oxford: Osprey, 2000, p. 3.
24. Geoffrey Hindley, *Medieval Sieges and Siegecraft*. New York: Skyhorse, 2009, p. 25.
25. Archer Jones, *The Art of War in the Western World*, p. 114.
26. John Burke, *Life in the Castle in Medieval England*. New York: Dorset, 1992, p. 75.
27. Quoted in Charles Coulson, *Castles in Medieval Society: Fortresses in England, France, and Ireland in the Central Middle Ages*. New York: Oxford University Press, 2003, p. 160.
28. Roy Ingleton, *Fortress Kent: The Guardian of England*. Barnsley, UK: Pen and Sword Military Press, 2012, p. 50.
29. Frances Gies and Joseph Gies, *Life in a Medieval Castle*. New York: Harper and Row, 1979, p. 20.
30. Hindley, *Medieval Sieges and Siegecraft*, p. 83.
31. Paul E. Chevedden, "The Invention of the Counterweight Trebuchet: A Study in Cultural Diffusion," in *Dumbarton Oaks Papers*,

no. 54, ed. Mary-Alice Talbot. Washington, DC: Dumbarton Oaks Research Library and Collection, 2000, p. 74.

32. Quoted in H.J. Nicholson, trans., *Chronicle of the Third Crusade: A Translation of the "Itinerarium Peregrinorum et Gesta Regis Ricardi."* Aldershot, UK: Ashgate, 1997, p. 213.

Chapter Four: Assaults by Sea

33. Prestwich, *Armies and Warfare in the Middle Ages*, p. 263.
34. Felipe Fernandez-Armesto, "Naval Warfare After the Viking Age, ca. 1100–1500," in Keen, *Medieval Warfare: A History*, p. 230.
35. Jones, *The Art of War in the Western World*, pp. 104–5.
36. Ian Heath, *The Vikings*. Oxford: Osprey, 2001, p. 31.

Chapter Five: Firearms Revolutionize War

37. Thomas F. Arnold, *The Renaissance at War*. London: Cassell, 2001, p. 16.
38. Arnold, *The Renaissance at War*, p. 16.
39. Arnold, *The Renaissance at War*, p. 16.
40. Quoted in Joseph Needham, *Science and Civilization in China: Military Technology*. New York: Cambridge University Press, 1986, p. 165.
41. Arnold, *The Renaissance at War*, p. 26.
42. Quoted in Hindley, *Medieval Sieges and Siegecraft*, p. 64.
43. Hindley, *Medieval Sieges and Siegecraft*, pp. 68–69.
44. John Julius Norwich, *Byzantium: The Decline and Fall*. New York: Knopf, 1996, p. 423.
45. John Keegan, *A History of Warfare*. New York: Random House, 1994, p. 320.

FOR FURTHER RESEARCH

Books

Matthew Bennett et al., *Fighting Techniques of the Medieval World: Equipment, Combat Skills and Tactics*. New York: Thomas Dunne, 2005.

Jane Bingham, *Internet-Linked Medieval World*. London: Usborne, 2012.

Brian T. Carie, *Warfare in the Medieval World*. South Yorkshire, UK: Pen and Sword, 2012.

David Crouch, *William Marshall: Knighthood, War, and Chivalry, 1147–1219*. New York: Pearson, 2010.

Stephen Currie, *The Medieval Castle*. San Diego: ReferencePoint, 2013.

Kelly Devries and Robert D. Smith, *Medieval Military Technology*. Toronto: University of Toronto Press, 2012.

Martin J. Dougherty, *The Medieval Warrior: Weapons, Technology, and Fighting Techniques, A.D. 1000–1500*. Guilford, CT: Lyons, 2011.

Frances Gies, *The Knight in History*. New York: HarperCollins, 2011.

Geoffrey Hindley, *Medieval Sieges and Siegecraft*. New York: Skyhorse, 2009.

Robert Jones, *Knight: The Warrior and World of Chivalry*. Oxford: Osprey, 2011.

Sean McGlynn, *By Sword and Fire: Cruelty and Atrocity in Medieval Warfare*. New Haven, CT: Phoenix, 2010.

David Nicolle, *European Medieval Tactics, 1260–1500*. Oxford, UK: Osprey, 2012.

Charles Oman, *A History of the Art of War in the Middle Ages*. Vol. 1. London: Acheron, 2012.

Lincoln Paine, *The Sea and Civilization: A Maritime History of the World*. New York: Knopf, 2013.

Clifford J. Rogers, *The Oxford Encyclopedia of Medieval Warfare and Military Technology*. New York: Oxford University Press, 2010.

Jeffrey L. Singman, *The Middle Ages: Everyday Life in Medieval Europe*. New York: Sterling, 2013.

Websites

The Longbow (www.themiddleages.net/longbow.html). An easy-to-read discussion of one of the most important weapons employed in medieval warfare.

Medieval History in the Movies (www.fordham.edu/Halsall/medfilms.asp#feudalism). This spirited and worthwhile overview of films set in the Middle Ages includes several movies depicting medieval warfare.

Medieval Warfare (www.hyw.com/books/history/Medi0000.htm). This worthwhile site is part of the authors' highly useful online overview of medieval times.

Medieval Weapons and Armor (www.medievalwarfare.info/weapons .htm). A visually beautiful presentation by James McDonald of the various kinds of armor and weapons used by medieval European knights and other soldiers, with excellent written descriptions of each.

Medieval Weapons and Armor (www.medievalwarfare.info/weapons .htm#bombards). A terrific site provided by Medieval Warfare Resources featuring fairly detailed definitions and descriptions of almost all the weapons and weapon systems used in Europe's Middle Ages.

The Swiss Pikeman (http://hubpages.com/hub/The-Swiss-Pikeman). This excellent overview of the famous military formations of Swiss soldiers wielding long pikes includes some colorful, accurately rendered paintings of these formations.

Training a Knight (www.medieval-life.net/knight_training.htm). A brief but informational synopsis of how a squire trained to become a knight.

William the Conqueror (www.themiddleages.net/people/william_con queror.html). A brief biography of the Norman leader who defeated the English at Hastings in 1066, ushering in a new era of medieval fortifications and warfare systems.

INDEX

PICTURE CREDITS

Cover: Ms 5089-90 Battle between Saracens and Christians during the Crusades, from 'Chroniques des empereurs' by David Aubert, 1462 (vellum), Brabant School, (15th century)/Bibliotheque de L'Arsenal, Paris, France/Archives Charmet/The Bridgeman Art Library

Maury Aaseng: 8

© Bettmann/Corbis: 45

© Heritage Images/Corbis: 18

© Lebrecht Music & Arts/Corbis: 65

Thinkstock Images: 4, 5, 52

The battle of Hastings, English School, (19th century)/Private Collection/© Look and Learn/The Bridgeman Art Library: 14

Various pikes, European, 15th–16th century (iron)/© Wallace Collection, London, UK/The Bridgeman Art Library: 22

Knights Templar, France, 12th century/De Agostini Picture Library/G. Dagli Orti/The Bridgeman Art Library: 27

Armor for Man and Horse with Völs-Colonna Arms, c.1575 (steel) , Italian School, (16th century)/Cleveland Museum of Art, OH, USA/John L. Severance Fund/The Bridgeman Art Library: 31

Roy 14 E IV f.23 The Siege of Mortagne, Vol III "From the Coronation of Richard II to 1387", by Jean de Batard Wavrin/British Library, London, UK/© British Library Board. All Rights Reserved/The Bridgeman Art Library: 37

Aerial view of Arundel Castle, showing the South Front, the Motte, the Keep and the Lower and Upper Baileys (photo),/His Grace The Duke of Norfolk, Arundel Castle/The Bridgeman Art Library: 41

Loading Goods on to a Ship, from the manuscript 'Justiniano Institutiones Feodorum et Alia', c.1300 (vellum), Bolognese School, (14th century)/Biblioteca Nazionale, Turin, Italy/Index/The Bridgeman Art Library: 49

Departure of a Boat for the Crusades, written in Galacian for Alfonso X (1221–84) (vellum), Spanish School, (13th century)/Biblioteca Monasterio del Escorial, Madrid, Spain/Giraudon/The Bridgeman Art Library: 56

Roger Bacon, the inventor of gunpowder, McConnell, James Edwin (1903–95) / Private Collection/© Look and Learn/The Bridgeman Art Library: 61

Armoured soldiers firing match-lock Arquebus, late 15th century (hand coloured woodcut), German School, (15th century)/Private Collection/Peter Newark Military Pictures/The Bridgeman Art Library: 68

ABOUT THE AUTHOR

Historian Don Nardo is best known for his books for young people about the ancient and medieval worlds. These include volumes on the histories, cultures, mythologies, arts, and literatures of the ancient inhabitants of Mesopotamia, Egypt, Greece, and Rome. Among his books about medieval times are studies of castles, warfare, arts and architecture, literature, religious pilgrimages, the Inquisition, the onset of the Black Death, the Viking invasions, and the trials of Joan of Arc and Galileo. Nardo also composes and arranges orchestral music. He lives with his wife, Christine, in Massachusetts.